theory for piano students

by **LORA BENNER**

**BOOK
FIVE**

ED. 2742

G. SCHIRMER, *Inc.*

DISTRIBUTED BY

HAL•LEONARD®
CORPORATION
7777 W. BLUEMOUND RD. P.O. BOX 13819 MILWAUKEE, WI 53213

Foreword

Theory 5 gives additional knowledge and experience in melody, harmony, rhythm, modulation, transposition, scales, phrases, and the Period Form.

Sections on modes, figures, motives, phrases, polyrhythms, and the use of theoretic knowledge in learning music have been included. Elementary composition is begun.

The scope of the material can be increased by additional work in each lesson; by examination of relatively easy material for all aspects of melody, harmony, and rhythm thus far explored; and by playing and transposing this material.

Suggested material: Easier compositions by Beethoven, Schubert, Tchaikovsky, Schumann, Mendelssohn, and Bartok.

Contents

Lesson One

TRIADS

Most of the music we play contains chords or parts of chords, solid or broken. Knowing them well is important.

There are several ways to identify chords.

1 Through their intervals
2 Through their accidentals
3 Through their scale degrees

1. Through their intervals:

A MAJOR triad has a major 3rd and a perfect 5th.

A MINOR triad has a minor 3rd and a perfect 5th.

A DIMINISHED triad has a minor 3rd and a diminished 5th.

An AUGMENTED triad has a major 3rd and an augmented 5th.

Complete the following intervals and triads according to the example. Then start with the root of each and sing each interval and triad as a melodic interval and triad. After you sing each one, play it on the piano to check your singing accuracy. Sing an octave lower or higher if the position is not in your singing range.

Example

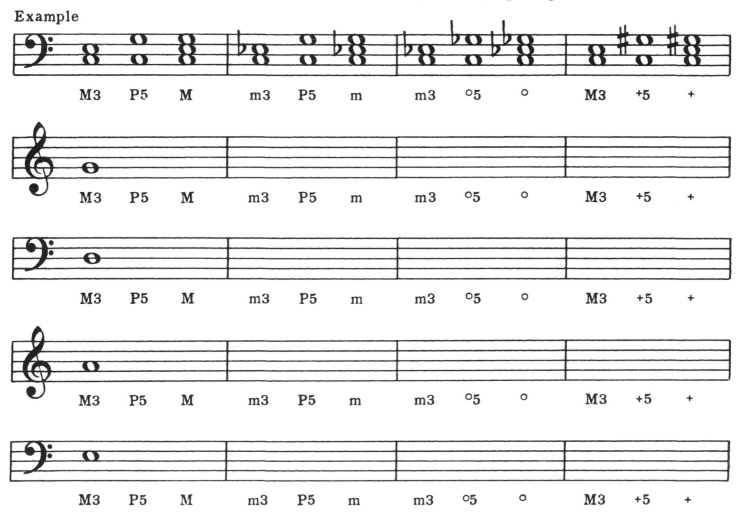

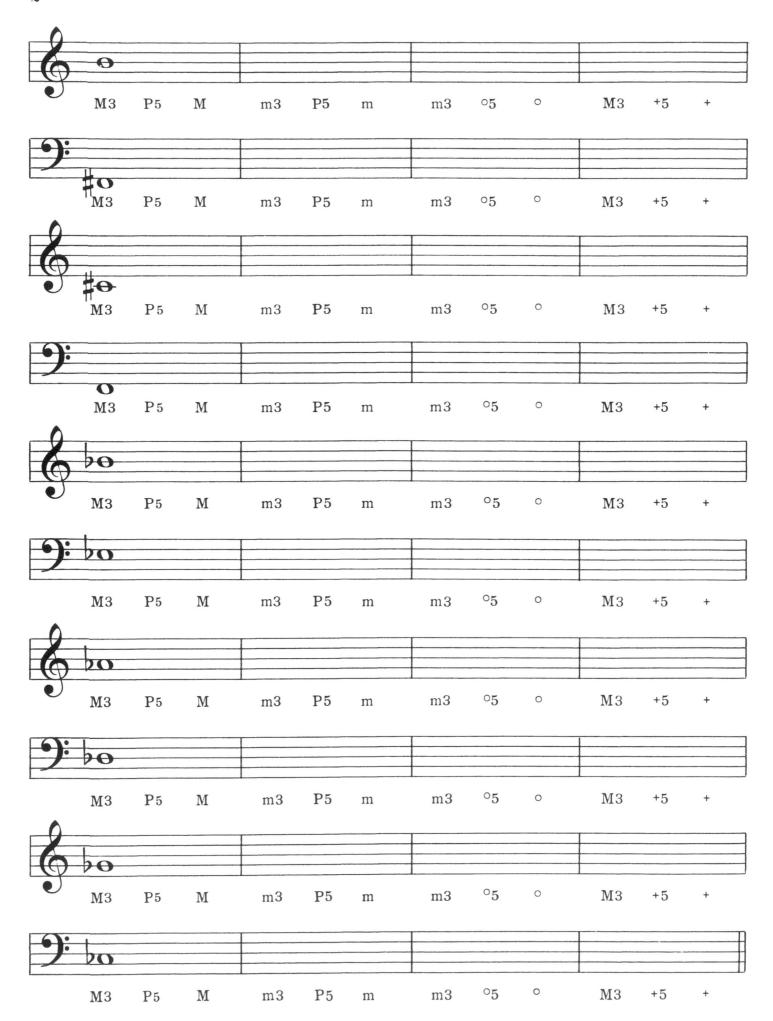

2. Through their accidentals:

     A MINOR triad lowers the 3rd of the Major triad a half-step.

     A DIMINISHED triad lowers the 5th of the Minor triad a half-step.

     An AUGMENTED triad raises the 5th of the Major triad a half-step.

Complete the following, then play them.

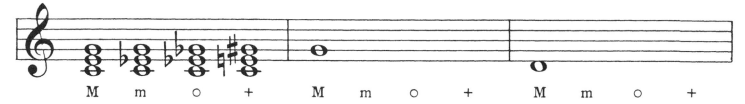

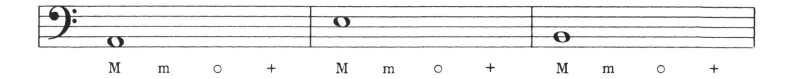

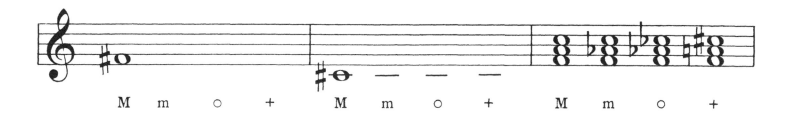

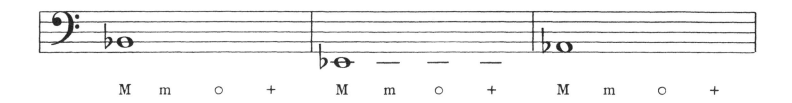

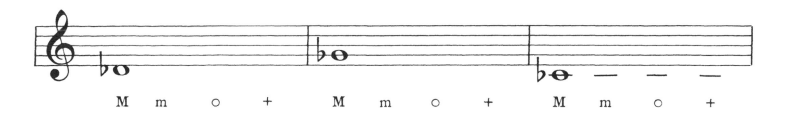

3 Through their scale degrees. This is called TONALITY.

The scale degrees are tones of certain keys.

Review the scales of triads on major and minor keys given below. Play them.

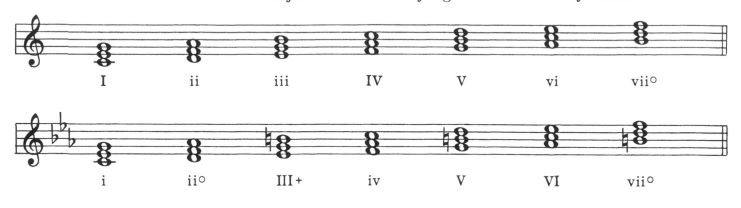

MAJOR TRIADS are   I   (1 - 3 - 5) of Major Keys

IV (4 - 6 - 8) of Major Keys

V (5 - 7 - 2) of Major and Harmonic Minor Keys

VI (6 - 1 - 3) of Harmonic Minor Keys

MINOR TRIADS are   II   (2 - 4 - 6) of Major Keys

III (3 - 5 - 7) of Major Keys

VI (6 - 1 - 3) of Major Keys

I (1 - 3 - 5) of Harmonic Minor Keys

IV (4 - 6 - 8) of Harmonic Minor Keys

DIMINISHED TRIADS are VII (7 - 2 - 4) of Major and Harmonic Minor Keys

II (2 - 4 - 6) of Harmonic Minor Keys

AUGMENTED TRIADS are III (3 - 5 - 7) of Harmonic Minor Keys

*The key of db minor has no key signature.

For the following: Put in the proper key signatures.

Write in the proper key name.

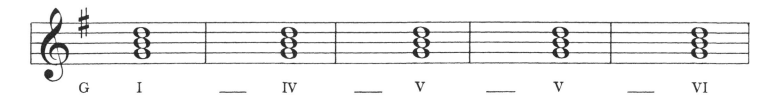

G   I   ___ IV   ___ V   ___ V   ___ VI

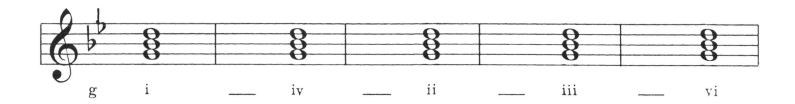

g   i   ___ iv   ___ ii   ___ iii   ___ vi

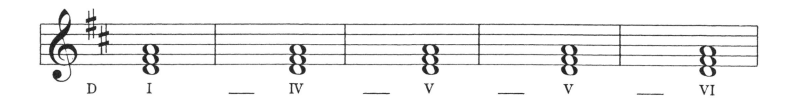

D   I   ___ IV   ___ V   ___ V   ___ VI

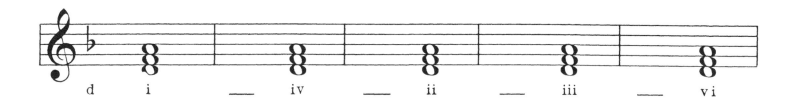

d   i   ___ iv   ___ ii   ___ iii   ___ vi

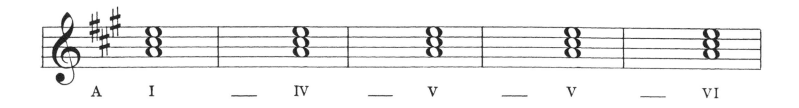

A   I   ___ IV   ___ V   ___ V   ___ VI

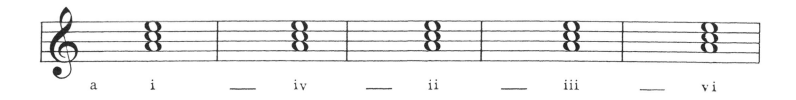

a   i   ___ iv   ___ ii   ___ iii   ___ vi

Work Sheet

1 Name three ways to identify triads.

    1 _____

    2 _____

    3 _____

2 On the following triads, add the accidentals necessary so that each set has a Major, a Minor, a Diminished and an Augmented triad:

3 Separate the intervals of the following triads and write below each, its type and size:

G Major
   Triad

G Minor
   Triad

G Diminished
   Triad

G Augmented
   Triad

F Major
   Triad

F Minor
   Triad

4 Write the scale of triads for D major on the staff below.

Write the scale degree for each root and the type of each triad.

5 Write the scale of triads for B minor on the staff below.

Write the scale degree for each root and the type of each triad.

6 What scale degrees of a Major key have Minor triads?_____

7 What scale degrees of a Minor key have Minor triads?_____

8 What scale degrees of a Major key have Major triads?_____

9 What scale degrees of a Minor key have Major triads?_____

10 What scale degrees of a Major and a Minor key have

Diminished Triads: Major?_____

Minor?_____

Augmented Triad? _____

Lesson Two

PHRASES and PERIOD FORM CONSTRUCTION

A PHRASE is the SMALLEST COMPLETE musical idea in music composition. It is similar to a sentence or a clause in sentence construction.

A PHRASE is the natural division of the melody and ends with a weak or strong cadence. A cadence is musical punctuation.

REGULAR phrases have four measures.

IRREGULAR phrases have less or more than four measures.

Home Sweet Home has regular phrases:

This is a one-part form since it is not the complete piece. (When a one-part form is the entire piece, it is called a PERIOD FORM.)

Henry R. Bishop

1. Write the Chord name on the lines below the chords.

2. Give the complete name of the cadences in

measures 3 - 4 _____

measures 7 - 8 _____

Play these two phrases, then transpose them to the keys of E, F, G, D and C through knowledge of each new key and the visual positions of the notes and intervals. The melody begins on *do,* goes up one step, then another with the lower third added, etc. The left hand has *do* in the bass (one octave below the melody) with the fifth above to start, etc.

There are TWO types of phrases:

ANTECEDENT (Question) phrase

CONSEQUENT (Answer) phrase

When the Antecedent and Consequent phrases are the same except for the cadence, they are called PARALLEL or in PARALLEL CONSTRUCTION.

The two phrases given for *Home Sweet Home* are parallel. The first phrase, the Antecedent, ends with an imperfect authentic cadence. The second phrase, the Consequent, ends with a perfect authentic cadence. It could have been written with a first and second ending:

Each phrase in music composition can be divided into two or more parts called motives.

A MOTIVE is the shortest part of a melody which makes musical sense. It has two or more notes. It is usually rhythmic as well as melodic.

Home Sweet Home has two motives within each phrase.

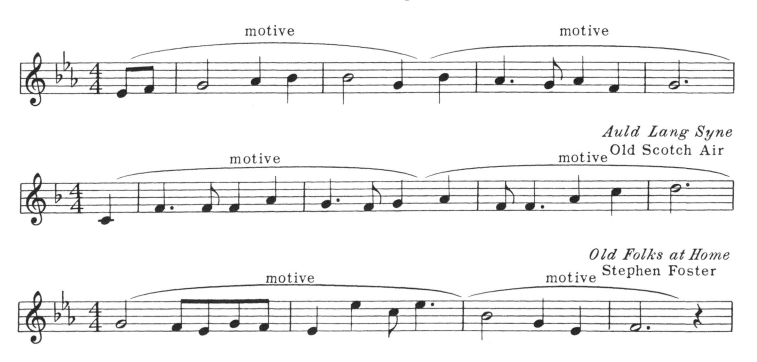

Auld Lang Syne
Old Scotch Air

Old Folks at Home
Stephen Foster

No Picnic?

Notice the Key Signature and the Time Signature.

1 Draw a slur over each of the two measure motives. They have similar patterns but are
   not identical since they have different notes.

2 Play the motives with your right hand. Notice that the first motive begins with C♭ *do*.
   The second motive begins with A♭ *la*.

3 Write the syllables below each note for the melody below.

4 Sing the melody using the syllables.

5 Write the Roman Numerals under the chords on the lines given.

6 Play *No Picnic?* through with both hands. Then play the first motive, hands separately,
   then together. See how few times you must play this in order to do it without the music.

   Play the second motive the same way, then the entire piece.
   Theoretic knowledge aids in understanding and memorizing compositions.

7 Transpose *No Picnic?* to other keys in the following order:

Major Keys: C, C♯, D, E♭, E, F, F♯
             B, B♭, A, A♭, G.

Minor Keys: C, D, E, F, G.

Composing Parallel Period Forms

There are many ways to write harmony for any melody. Below are a few simple treatments for chords.

Solid   Split   Broken

Here is a melody. Copy it on the top lines of the grandstaff below and add I, V or V7 chords for the left hand on the lower lines. Use whatever chord treatment you wish.

Transpose this little piece into other major and minor keys.

On the grandstaff below, compose your own melody and harmony. Use I, V or V7 chords in any treatment you wish. Then transpose your piece to other major and minor keys.

Chord knowledge is important even though we do not spell out the chords in everything we study. Much of chord knowledge should become automatic. There are times when thinking of the chord names helps in memorizing music. When this knowledge is used in conjunction with finding motives and phrases and identifying cadences, memorizing is often easier to do and the results more lasting.

Norse Song by Robert Schumann is a two-part form or Binary form composition. The first part is given below.

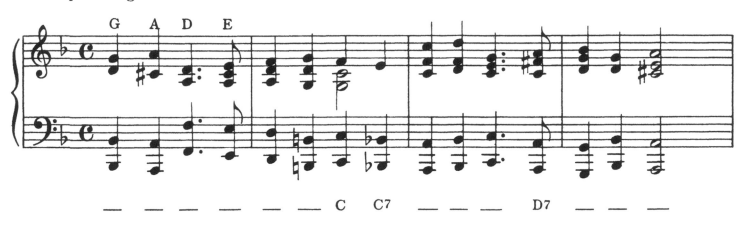

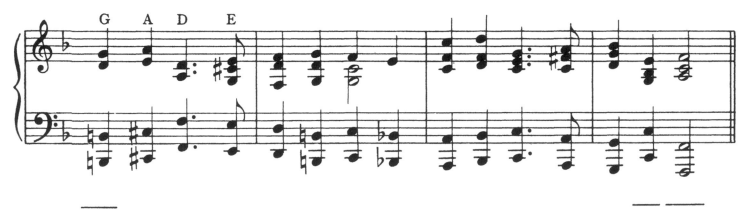

1 In what key is *Norse Song?* _____

2 What is the Time Signature? _____

3 How many phrases are there in this part? _____

4 Mark the two motives of the first phrase.

5 Are the phrases regular _____ or irregular _____ ?

6 Write the names of the chords on the lines below them. Use capital letters for Major and small letters for minor chords.

7 Play through slowly.

Work Sheet

1 What is a PHRASE? _____

_____

2 What punctuation ends a phrase? _____

3 How many measures are in a REGULAR phrase? _____

4 How many measures in an IRREGULAR phrase? _____

5 What are the two types of phrases called?

_____ (_____)

_____ (_____)

6 What is PARALLEL CONSTRUCTION?

_____

_____

7 What is a Motive? _____

_____

_____

8 How many notes are in a motive? _____

9 Name two characteristics of motives.

_____

_____

Lesson Three

Seventh Chords

A MAJOR 7th chord has M3, P5, and M7 - or, said another way,
　　　　　a Major triad plus a Major 7th interval.

A MINOR 7th chord has m3, P5, and m7 - or
　　　　　a Minor triad plus a Minor 7th interval.

A DOMINANT 7th chord has M3, P5, and m7 - or
　　　　　a Major triad plus a Minor 7th interval.

A HALF-DIMINISHED chord has m3, ○5, and m7 - or
　　　　　a Diminished triad and a Minor 7th interval.

A DIMINISHED 7th chord has m3, ○5, and ○7 - or
　　　　　a Diminished triad plus a Diminished 7th.

Using the note given as the lowest note (root) of the 7th, build, on the staffs below, the
　　　listed seventh chords. Play them.

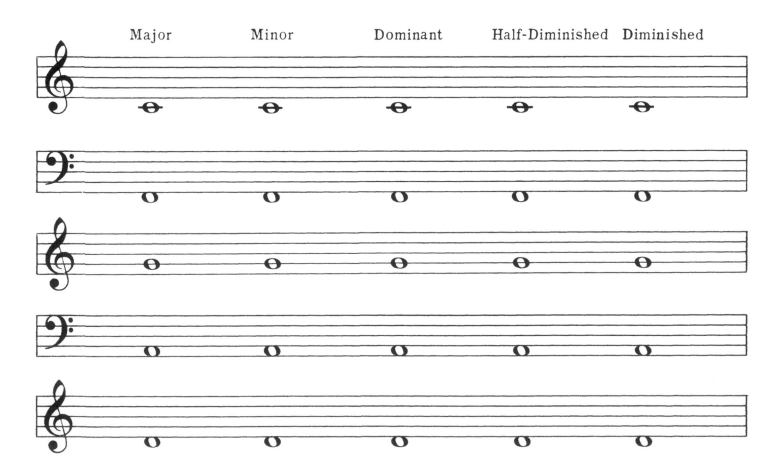

Study and play the 7ths on tones of the Major Scale below.

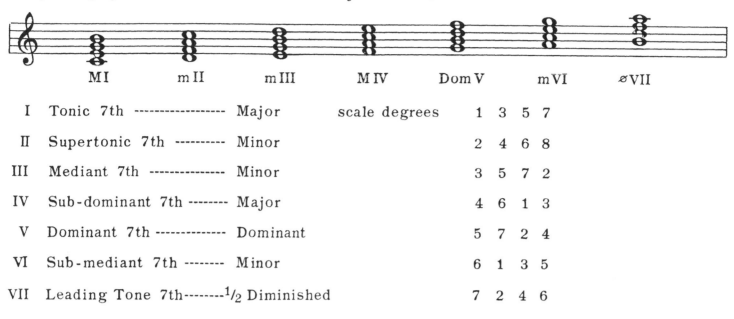

| MI | m II | m III | M IV | Dom V | m VI | ⌀VII |

I	Tonic 7th ----------------- Major	scale degrees	1	3	5	7
II	Supertonic 7th ---------- Minor			2	4	6	8
III	Mediant 7th -------------- Minor			3	5	7	2
IV	Sub-dominant 7th -------- Major			4	6	1	3
V	Dominant 7th ------------- Dominant			5	7	2	4
VI	Sub-mediant 7th -------- Minor			6	1	3	5
VII	Leading Tone 7th--------$1/2$ Diminished			7	2	4	6

Write the Major scales of 7ths and list the types and scale degrees below the chords. Use accidentals rather than key signatures. Play these and other scales of 7ths.

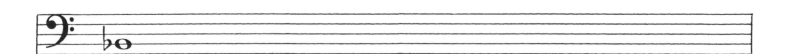

Name the scale degree with Roman numeral and type of seventh chord under each seventh given below. All are Major Keys. Play these 7ths.

Write seventh chords above the Roman numeral in the keys given on the staff below, use accidentals. Then play the 7ths.

Key of G	Key of B	Key of E	Key of A	Key of F	Key of D

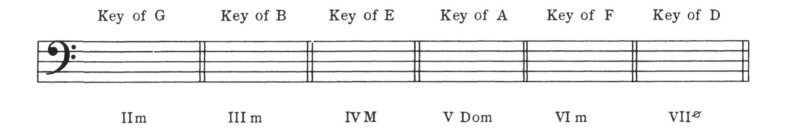

II m	III m	IV M	V Dom	VI m	VII⌀

The **DIMINISHED** 7th chord is not found in the major scale of sevenths. It is built on the leading tone of the harmonic minor scale. The scale degrees are 7 2 4 6 of the harmonic minor.

The **ROOT** of the diminished seventh chord is **ALWAYS** an accidental. It is the altered tone which is added to the **NATURAL** minor to make the **HARMONIC** minor with the half-step between 7-8, *ti* and *do*.

Write in the key signature, the *do,* and the ○7 chords on the staff below for the minor keys given. Here are two examples:

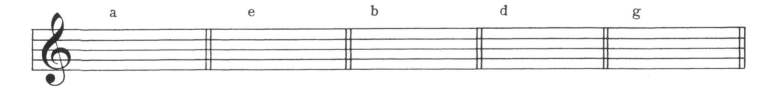

Play the ○7 chord for every harmonic minor key.

The DOMINANT 7th chord is the MOST IMPORTANT 7th chord.

It is the same for a MAJOR KEY and its parallel HARMONIC MINOR.

Play the I V I and I V7 I chords below. Play them in all Major and Harmonic Minor Keys.

The Dominant 7th is used when a stronger pull to the next harmony is desired. By adding
the interval of the 7th, which is a DISSONANT interval, the consonant dominant triad
becomes a dissonant 7th chord which pulls for resolution.

RESOLUTION – a consonant which follows a dissonant.

Play the following dominant 7th chords. Observe the rests. Let your ear hear the resolution
before you play it, then play it.

WRITING the 7th chord 2nd, remember two things:

1 The LOWER note is placed on the LEFT $(L = L)$ and is the chord seventh.
   The Upper note is placed on the Right and is the chord root.

2 The notes on the proper side of the stem are lined up with the notes on the other staff.

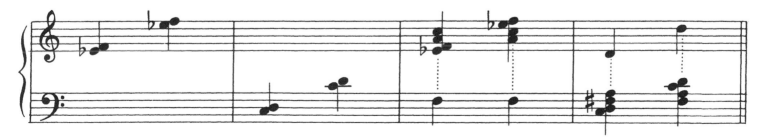

The DOMINANT 7th is often used in MODULATION. Play the following slowly and carefully. This is the DOMINANT MODULATION CIRCLE. The Dominant Circle of Scales moves clockwise. The Dominant Circle of Modulation moves counter-clockwise.

Play this several times until it is familiar.

There are many ways to use the Dominant 7th chord for modulation. Some of these ways are:

Start from any key to any other key on the modulating circle. When the desired new key is reached, play the extended authentic cadence in the new key to establish it.

Play the following modulation:

Now either from memory or reading the modulating circle on page 18, start at G and go to B♭. Then establish B♭ by playing the extended authentic cadence.

Modulate from various keys to various other keys in this way to become familiar with this type of modulation.

Play the following circle of Dominant 7ths several times.

Now start with any Major or Minor tonic triad, play the dominant 7th by adding a minor 7th to the major triad. Then play through the dominant 7ths until reaching the desired new key. Play the tonic triad of the new key – either major or minor – and the extended authentic cadence in the new key. This is direct dominant modulation.

Work Sheet

1 On the staff below, write the Major scale of 7ths and write the type below each one:

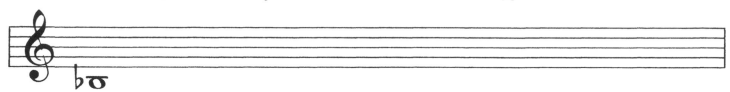

2 Complete the following chart:

TRIAD	+	7th INTERVAL	=	SEVENTH type
Major		_____		_____
Major		_____		_____
Minor		_____		_____
Diminished		_____		_____
Diminished		_____		_____

3 Which is the most important 7th chord? _____

4 In which two scales is it found? _____

_____

5 Play the following modulation:

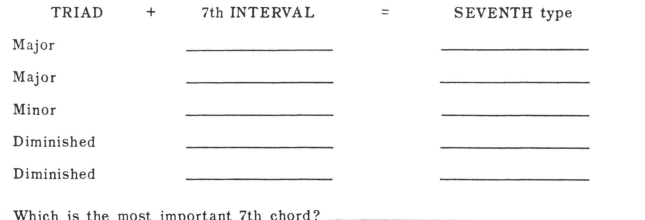

6 Write this modulation from C7 to the established key of Eb Major.

Lesson Four
Figures - Parallel Construction of Minor Period Forms

FIGURES are the smallest unit in music composition. They are tiny musical ideas. Sometimes a motive will contain two or more figures as in Beethoven *Sonata Opus 49, No. 2:*

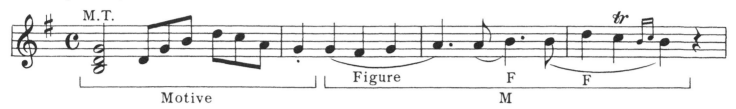

In the Rondo of Beethoven's *Sonata Opus 49, No. 1*, the first motive is made up of two similar figures: (M.T. means main theme.)

The following is the beginning of study number 22, Opus 50 by Cornelius Gurlitt.

You can feel the place where the first motive ends and the next one begins although the patterns or figures are similar.

There are many compositions where there is no such feeling during the entire phrase. The figure and the motive are the same. When the motive is a figure which is repeated, this is often called a figure rather than a motive because it is a musical pattern.

Here is part of study number 23 also from Opus 50 by Gurlitt.

The following are from numbers 2 and 5, Opus 24 by Giuseppe Concone.

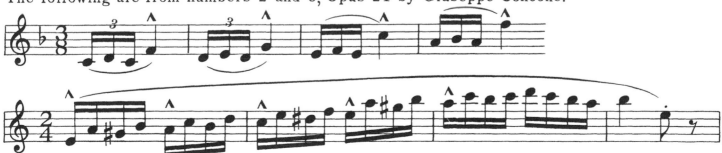

The following short composition from *Music for Piano Students* uses the I and IV chords of F♯ minor. Play this.

Ireland

Let us see what can be learned about this short piece.

1 The KEY SIGNATURE - 3 ♯s probably means either A Major or F♯ Minor. The final chord has F♯ in the soprano and bass; so we assume the key to be F♯ Minor. But there is no E♯ for the Harmonic form; so we assume it to be in the Natural Minor.

2 The TIME SIGNATURE - 4 beats to a measure with a ♩ = one beat. The melody begins on beat 4 as do all the three figures; so we conclude the meter to be 4, 1, 2, 3 and count this way.

3 The FORM - There are first and second endings; so the phrases are parallel. There are two - four measure phrases; so they are regular. There are three figures with the same rhythm.

4 The CONSTRUCTION - the first two figures end with *mi* which is *do* for the relative major. The second two figures end with F♯ *do*. The melody has a six note span. The melody moves scalewise for two measures.

5 The HARMONY is I, IV, I, IV and I, IV, I, I.

Now play *IRELAND* again. Then transpose it to other minor keys. Play it in F♯ MAJOR and transpose it to other major keys.

On the staffs below, compose a Period Form in parallel construction in a minor key. Select a simple melodic rhythm and no more than a six note melodic span. Use only the I and IV chords for harmony.

On the staff below, *Ireland* has been transposed to A natural minor; a new chord has been added to the harmony, and two chords are in each measure except in measure eight.

Play this as written, then in F# minor and other minor keys.

Now play it in A major and other major keys.

Using staves below, write your composition adding a different chord in measure two or three and with two chords to each measure except the eighth. Write it first in a minor then in a major key. Then play it and transpose it to other minor and major keys.

The pattern of the left hand for the first two full measures may be repeated to form an OSTINATO bass.

An OSTINATO bass, also called a GROUND bass, is a *rhythmic, melodic figure* which is *repeated* throughout a composition or maintained for a definite part of it.

Play this figure.

The following part of *March of the Little Toy Soldiers* (also called, *March of the Little Lead Soldiers*) by Gabriel Pierné has sections of ground bass.

The earliest examples of ostinato are found in motets of the 13th century. It was used during the Baroque period. Many composers of the 20th century are reviving the Ostinato or Ground bass.

It is also used in Jazz improvization. The ostinato bass here can be used to provide a steady background for a free display of the imagination in the right hand.

Boogie has a GROUND bass with a definite Harmonic pattern:

I I IV I V IV I I

There are a great many possibilities for varying the rhythmic and melodic patterns of the ground bass in Boogie.

Work Sheet

1 The following is an eight measure adaptation of the Boogie bass with the pattern from the second version of *Ireland*. The melody is taken from the top four measures of page 25.

Play this. Transpose it to two other keys.

2 Write either an eight measure Boogie or a piece, using the bass from your composition on page 23 to form the pattern. You may use the same melody idea if you wish, but make it sound right with the ground bass.

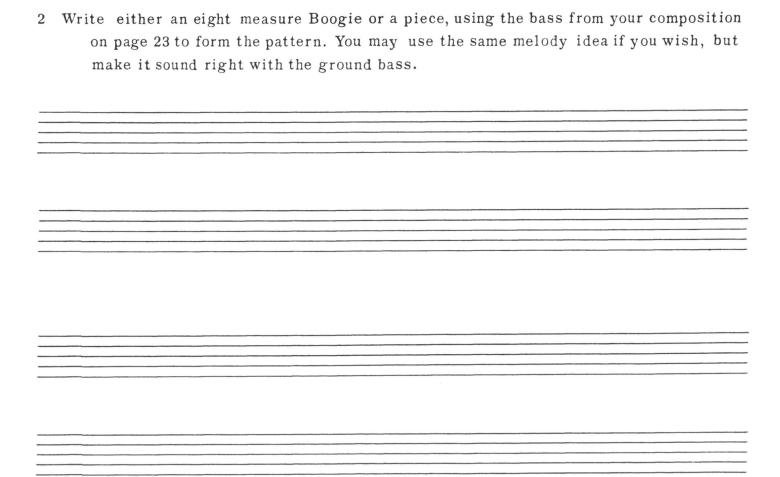

Lesson Five

Scales and Modes

Early in the 17th century, musicians began to use Major and Minor scales for most compositions.

Before this time, music was composed on other diatonic scales called MODES.
(Dia = through, Tonic = tone – one of each letter tone.)

The MODES were used in church music and were called church modes until French musicians began to give them the Greek names by which they are now called.

Each white key on the piano is *do* for a different diatonic MODE.

Each mode has its own system of whole and half-steps which can be transposed just as the scale of C is transposed by starting the whole and half-step pattern with another note as *do*.

From C to C is the IONIAN MODE (C major scale) with half-steps 3-4, 7-8.

From D to D is the DORIAN MODE with half-steps between 2-3, 6-7.

From E to E is the PHRYGIAN MODE with half-steps between 1-2, 5-6.

× = Characteristic Tone

From F to F is the LYDIAN MODE with half-steps between 4-5, 7-8.

From G to G is the MIXOLYDIAN MODE with half-steps between 3-4, 6-7.

From A to A is the AEOLIAN MODE (Natural Minor Scale) with half-steps 2-3, 5-6.

From B to B is the LOCRIAN MODE with half-steps 1-2, 4-5.

Each MODE has a CHARACTERISTIC TONE which makes it different from a Major or Minor scale (except the Ionian and Aeolian which are the Major and natural Minor scales).

DORIAN raises the 6th tone B. B♭ would be the D Natural Minor.

PHRYGIAN lowers the 2nd tone F. F♯ would be the E Natural Minor.

LYDIAN raises the 4th tone B. B♭ would be the F Major Scale.

MIXOLYDIAN lowers the 7th tone F. F♯ would be the G Major Scale.

Modern composers are frequently using Modes as the basis for their compositions. There are three reasons for this:

1 16th century modal music is being imitated.
2 Slavic and other modal music influence is growing.
3 The use of systems other than classical harmony based on the Ionian Mode and its relative minor, affords more variety.

TONALITY means the composition is based on the tones of a scale.

MODALITY means the composition is based on the tones of a mode.

Although the C major scale and its transpositions are modes, the two terms are maintained for clarity.

DORIAN MODE   AEOLIAN MODE (Natural Minor)

1 Write in the five missing Natural Minor Scales with the proper key signature for each.
2 Slur the half-steps for both modes.
3 Play both columns vertically, then horizontally.

30

PHRYGIAN MODE   AEOLIAN MODE - Natural Minor Scale

1 Complete the Aeolian Modes (Natural Minor Scales) with accidentals or with key signatures.
2 Slur the half-steps for both modes.
3 Play both columns vertically, then horizontally.

Dorian Modal Mood

Phrygian Fantasy March

Play these two short pieces. Then write a short period form piece in either the Dorian or Phrygian mode on the staffs below. Use I, IV - I, V - or I, IV, V chords for the harmony.

32

LYDIAN MODE

IONIAN MODE - Major Scale

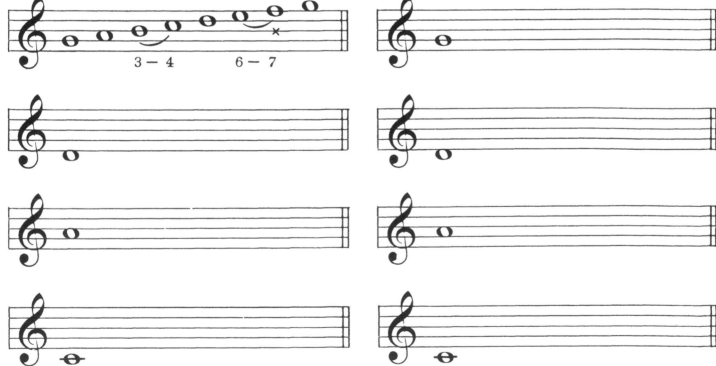

MIXOLYDIAN MODE

IONIAN MODE - Major Scale

1 Complete the MODES in both columns. Use accidentals.
2 Slur the half-steps for both modes.
3 Play both columns vertically, then horizontally.

Transposition of the Modes to any Signature

Ionian	*do*	=	1	(tonic) of transposed C scale
Dorian	*do*	=	2	(supertonic)
Phrygian	*do*	=	3	(mediant)
Lydian	*do*	=	4	(sub-dominant)
Mixolydian	*do*	=	5	(dominant)
Aeolian	*do*	=	6	(sub-mediant)

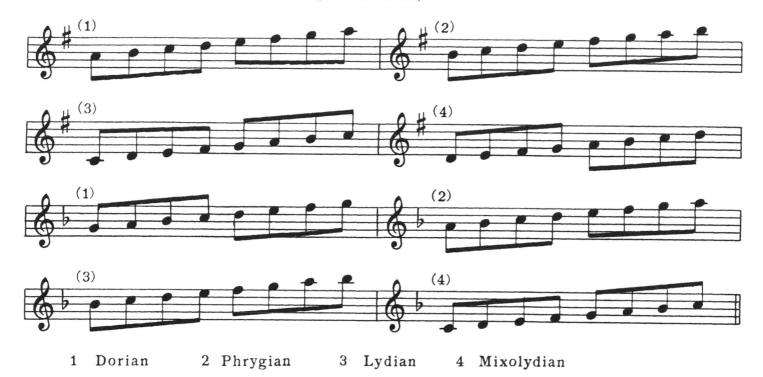

1 Dorian   2 Phrygian   3 Lydian   4 Mixolydian

The **WHOLE-TONE SCALE** has six tones each a whole-step apart.

There are only two whole-tone scales possible:
    C D E F♯ G♯ A♯ C and C♯ D♯ F G A B C♯

Each of these forms a whole-step circle so that any tone of either group may be *do* for the group of which it is a part. Debussy and others used this scale.

The **CHROMATIC SCALE** has twelve tones each a half-step apart.

There is only one chromatic scale possible.

Music written on this scale is called Twelve-Tone and is lacking in feeling for any key. Another name for this is Atonal (no one tone as a tonic).

This music is the most dissonant and far from classic harmony. Schönberg, or Schoenberg (changed after he moved to America) was one of the founders of this idea.
    Twelve Short Piano Pieces in 12 Tone Technique by Ernst Krenek.
    Twenty-Three Pieces for Children in 12 Tone Style by Julius Schloss.
    Twenty-Three Studies for Children in 12 Tone Style by Julius Schloss.

Chromatic HARMONY is the use of harmony in keys other than the diatonic scale on which the composition is written. Chopin and other romantic period composers used Chromatic Harmony.

The **PENTATONIC SCALE** has five tones. There is one scale C D F G A which can be transposed to C♯ D♯ F♯ G♯ A♯. A different modal treatment results when tones other than C or C♯ are used for *do*. The right hand of *Sunlight in a Clearing* is Pentatonic.

Sunlight in a Clearing

Play one octave higher than written

Work Sheet

1 For each of the following: (1) Write the mode one octave. (2) Mark the half-steps with slurs. (3) Put an X to show the CHARACTERISTIC Tone. (4) Write the half-step scale degrees on the lines.

DORIAN   Half-steps _____ , _____

PHRYGIAN   Half-steps _____ , _____

LYDIAN   Half-steps _____ , _____

MIXOLYDIAN   Half-steps _____ , _____

2 Write the two WHOLE-TONE Scales.

3 Write the PENTATONIC Scale and its TRANSPOSITION

Lesson Six

RHYTHM

RHYTHM in music is every use of TIME for sound or rests.

RHYTHM has four qualities:

TEMPO   METER   PATTERN   ACCENT (Agogic)

TEMPO: The SPEED or PACE, such as the metronome marking.

METER: the TIME VALUES for each measure. This is the number of beats in a measure and the type of note which gets one beat. Also called the TIME SIGNATURE.

See Theory for Piano Students, Book Two, page 18

The DYNAMIC ACCENTS for each measure

REGULAR

Simple time is also called BINARY because it is divisible by 2.
Compound time is called TERNARY because it is divisible by 3.

PATTERN is the grouping of notes and the rhythmic phrasing.

A REGULAR pattern has the beats or pulses divided normally:

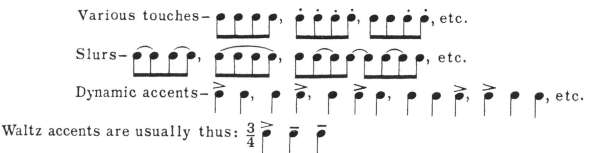

An IRREGULAR pattern does not divide the beats or pulses normally:

RHYTHMIC PHRASING is by means of

Waltz accents are usually thus:

Waltz

Cornelius Gurlitt Opus 101, No. 11

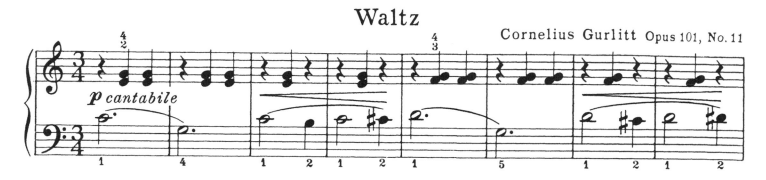

Country Dance

Franz Schubert Opus 171, No. 1

However, composers may redirect the accent thus:

Waltz

Peter Tchaikovsky Opus 39, No. 8

The **MAZURKA** is a dance in ¾ time often with the following pattern and with the accent on the third beat:

Mazurka

Frédéric Chopin Op. 68, No. 2

Lento ♩=116

Occasionally the accent falls on the second beat:

Mazurka

Frédéric Chopin Op. 63, No. 3

Allegretto

Chopin was the first composer to use this dance form as a basis for repertoire or program music. Chopin also based parts of some of the Mazurkas on MODES. This was the first of the modern use of modes in composition.

The **SARABANDE** is a stately dance from around 1600 and 1700. In slow triple meter (³⁄₂ time), it usually begins on beat one with the accent on beat two through an accented note or a longer value note.

Sarabande
from: Suite XI

George Frideric Handel

Andante lento

The POLONAISE is a Polish National dance, also stately. It is in a moderate triple meter. This dance was used at court ceremonies, not as a folk dance. Its first known use was in the late 1500s.

The earliest examples of the Polonaise in the form it now has were composed by Johann Sebastian Bach and are found in many of his Suites.

Polonaise

Johann Sebastian Bach

Clap or tap the rhythm of the above *Polonaise*.

A frequent pattern and accent for the Polonaise is

Polonaise

Frêdéric Chopin Op.40, No.1

The GIGUE is a rapid dance usually found as the closing piece of a Suite. Handel and Bach wrote many Gigues. The meter is compound and the style usually a fugue.

Gigues should be played with a strong, non-legato touch for the short value note patterns.

Gigue

George Frideric Handel

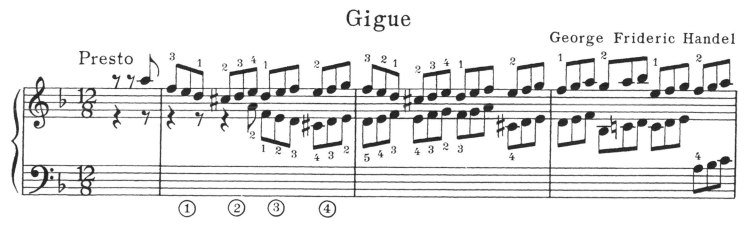

Count for the dotted note value in compound meter.

AGOGIC ACCENTS are important in rhythm. Agogic accents affect the tempo and are often shown by such words as *accelerando, ritardando, rallentando, tempo rubato* and *fermata.*

The deviation from a strict tempo is most important in phrasing and the intelligent playing of phrases.

The example below is from Gurlitt Opus 107, No. 9 and uses the *ritardando* and the *fermata.*

METRIC ACCENT is usually a steady beat of the meter. (Mendelssohn Opus 53 No. 4 Songs Without Words, etc.).

Notice that this phrase is in the PHRYGIAN MODE.

VOLUME ACCENT is the use of a chord with a single note or series of single notes. The feeling of thickness is a rhythmic as well as an harmonic device. Brahms was particularly fond of this accent.

Intermezzo

Johannes Brahms, Op. 116, No. 5

PATTERN ACCENT is the use of repeated patterns for emphasis.

Tarantella

Presto ♩.= 144   Felix Mendelssohn Opus 102, No. 3

1   What do these eight measures form? _____

2   How many phrases are in these eight measures? _____

3   Are they parallel? _____ or similar? _____

4   What kind of cadence is a I-V cadence? _____
       (*Theory for Piano Students,* Book Four, Page **17** or **48**)

5   Write the Roman Numerals on the lines under the cadence chords.

PITCH ACCENT is the use of a very high or very low note away from the pitch of the
      body of that section of a composition.

There are many examples of this pitch accent throughout music literature.

HARMONIC ACCENT is the use of a dissonant chord on a pulse or beat.

Prelude

Frédéric Chopin Opus 28, No. 7

The above phrase from *Prélude, Op. 28, No. 7* by Frédéric Chopin uses the harmonic accent.
    There is also an agogic accent in the last measure given here, as most artists
    lengthen the time of the first two beats.

EMBELLISHMENT - the use of mordents, appoggiaturas, trills, etc.

Mazurka

Moderato animato ♩ = 138   Frédéric Chopin Opus 67, No. 4

POLYRHYTHM

POLYRHYTHM is the use of contrasting rhythms.

Playing two against three or three against four to find the proper playing spacing for
  each note requires finding a common denominator.

For example, for two againt three, both two and three go into six. Therefore, six is the
  number used for each.

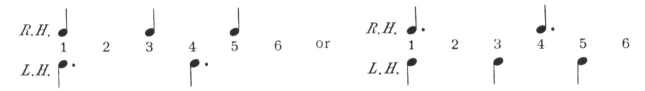

Tap both of these examples slowly and count. Then increase the speed— or tempo.

Now change from counting 1, 2, 3, 4, 5, 6 to one and two and three, then one two and three;
  or try saying NOT VER-Y HARD or NOT DIFF-I-CULT, while tapping.

Two against three is often found in $\frac{4}{4}$ time.

Play the following slowly, then increase tempo.

Feeling the rhythm is important. Set a slow metronome beat; play one hand, then the other hand, then both together without counting.

Three against four has a common number - twelve.

Tap and count the following:

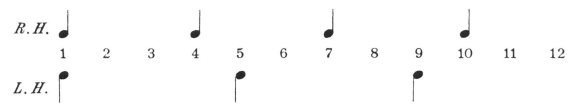

Tap this again but say—Both 1 2 Right Left 1 Right 1 Left Right 1 2
or Both ta ta Right Left ta Right ta Left Right ta ta

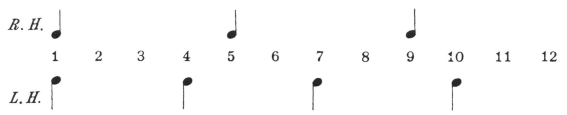

Tap this again but say—Both 1 2 Left Right 1 Left 1 Right Left 1 2
or Both ta ta Left Right ta Left ta Right Left ta ta

Now change from counting and say NOT VER-Y DIFF-I-CULT .

It is difficult to count three against four or larger numbers of notes against other larger
numbers of notes in this way while playing. Try playing the three to a beat with one
hand. Then play four to the same beat with the other hand. Then play them together
as was done separately.

Play the following slowly. Then increase the tempo.

Do this also with the metronome and without counting. Hands separately, then together.

Work Sheet

1 Name the 4 qualities of RHYTHM

_____   _____

_____   _____

2 Mark the accents for the following. Put in the time signatures.

3 Why is simple time called BINARY? _____

_____

4 Why is compound time called TERNARY? _____

_____

5 What is a METRIC ACCENT? _____

_____

6 What is a PATTERN ACCENT? _____

7 What is a PITCH ACCENT? _____

_____

8 Mark notes above and below the figures for R H 3 to L H 2

     1   2   3   4   5   6

9 Mark notes above and below the figures for R H 3 to L H 4

    1 2 3 4 5 6 7 8 9 10 11 12

10 What does AGOGIC ACCENT affect? _____

Lesson Seven
THEORETIC KNOWLEDGE AND USE

The basic musical idea or ideas for sonatinas and sonatas is called a THEME. There are usually two themes in the Sonata-Allegro movement, a Main Theme and a Second Theme.

The Motives within these themes are very important as these are used in the DEVELOPMENT section in various ways.

Sonata

Ludwig van Beethoven Opus 49, No.1

The Second Theme is used in different ways in the Development section:

The Main Theme of the Rondo of the same Sonata contains a pattern Beethoven uses in

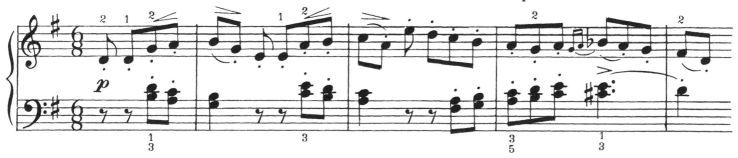

many of his compositions in many different ways. Play the last three notes of the first partial measure with your right hand and end with the first note in the second measure (first full measure) – the *How Dry I Am* theme.

SUBJECT is also used instead of THEME for many of the Baroque compositions. The following is a SUBJECT of a Handel Sonata.

Learning Study No. 20, Opus 50 by Cornelius Gurlitt (Romantic Period composer, 1820-1901)

Il basso sempre legato e tranquillo

Number all the measures on this page.

1 What is the Key Signature? _____ Key? _____ Time Signature? _____

2 Look over Part One. Regular phrases? _____   How many? _____

       Cadences - Measures 3 - 4 _____   7 - 8 _____

       Melody mainly scale - wise? _____

3 Look over Part Two. Measures 9 - 16 Regular Phrases? _____

       Cadence in measures 15 - 16 is in the Key of B.

       Name the two chords and tell type of cadence.

     Measures 17 - 24 are an *episode* based on the melody in meas. 9 - 10. They return

       to the signature Key of E.

     Measures 25 - 28 restate the THEME (melody of first phrase)

     Measures 29 - 33 are an *extension* of measure 28

     Measures 34 - 35 are the perfect authentic cadence at the end of Part Two.

     Measures 35 - 49 are the CODA.

4 Continue writing the chord names under the blocked chord version below.

5 Play this version until it is familiar.

6 Learn the piece. This means learn to play it properly and by memory. Learn a phrase at
   a time, sing and count the melody to yourself each time you play. Always use good
   dynamics.

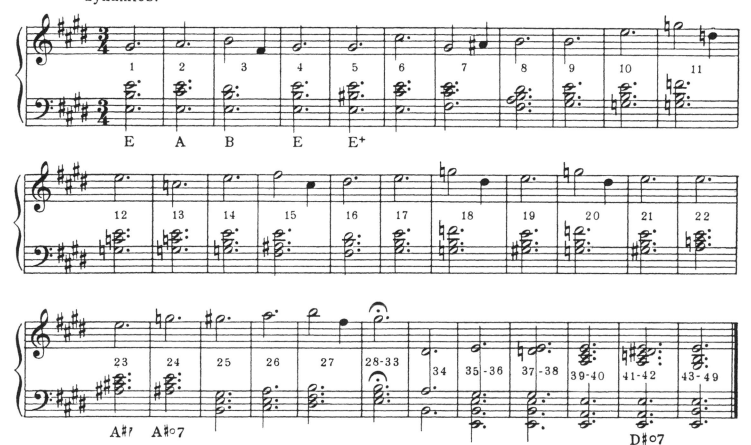

A PHRASE is the shortest COMPLETE musical idea. A phrase ends with a CADENCE.

A REGULAR phrase has 4 measures. There are also many IRREGULAR phrases in music.
The following is Béla Bartók's Book 2 No.1, *For Children*. It has a 5 measure phrase.

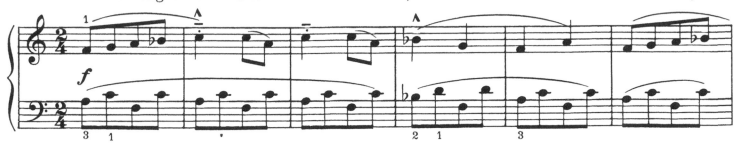

The following is *A Loss* by Gurlitt. It has 8 measure phrases.

When measures are long with many short value notes, phrases may be shorter. When measures have few notes of long values, phrases may be longer.

It is not always easy to locate the phrases — to find the end of one and the beginning of
the next one — particularly in contemporary music. Modern composers disguise the
cadences by unusual harmonies or by not having a definite rest spot for the cadences.

When the melody is complex with many notes and intricate rhythms, the harmony is likely
to be simpler with less chord change.

When there is a great deal of harmonic change, the melody is likely to be simpler.

The melody may be chord tones, chord tones with non-harmonic notes, or scale tones.

Lesson Eight
COMPOSITION

Look over the following melody carefully, then play it through. Write in the following:

(1) Key Signature   (2) Time Signature   (3) Chord names on lines

(4) Cadences for measures 4 and 8 in Roman Numerals.

(5) Write a single bass note to go with each chord. It will usually be the root, but not always. Check to see what sounds best. Use accidentals if you need them.

(6) What kind of dance is it? _____

Cadences ___ ___   ___ ___

Now compose an original melody to fit with the same chords in the Left Hand. Write the melody in single notes, but they do not have to belong to the chord. Use anything which sounds good to you.

Here are three melodies for Period Form composition. Write in the time signatures. On lines
4 and 5, compose original melody or melodies. Then select one of the five melodies
and copy it on the lower staves and add harmony.

Play your composition and transpose it to major and minor keys and to the Dorian and Phrygian modes. (For Dorian, play one note higher than written. For Phrygian, play two
notes higher than written. But use the same key signature.)

Examination

1 Name three ways to identify chords.

By their _____   _____

_____

2 Write the following intervals and triads on D:

    M3 P5 M   m3 P5 m   m3 o5 o   M3 +5 +

3 Write the kind of triad under each of the following:

_____   _____   _____   _____   _____   _____

4 What triads are MAJOR in a MAJOR KEY? _____
    Give Roman Numerals.

        MAJOR in a MINOR KEY? _____

        MINOR in a MAJOR KEY? _____

        MINOR in a MINOR KEY? _____

Give the Roman numerals for DIMINISHED triads:

    MAJOR KEY _____   MINOR KEY _____

Where is the AUGMENTED triad found?

On _____ of a _____ Key

5 Name the two types of PHRASES.

_____ and _____

How many measures in a REGULAR phrase? _____

What is a FIGURE? _____

What is a MOTIVE? _____

_____

What is a PHRASE? _____

_____

6 Name the intervals in the following:

a MAJOR 7th _____

a MINOR 7th _____

a DOMINANT 7th _____

a HALF-DIMINISHED 7th _____

a DIMINISHED 7th _____

Write the type of 7th under each chord on the staff below:

_____ _____ _____ _____ _____ _____ _____   _____

7 For the following 4 measures by Gurlitt, tell

What kind of a phrase? _____

In what key is it? _____

Under each chord, write the name. Write Cadence Scale degrees in Roman numerals.

_____ _____ _____ _____ _____ _____ _____ _____

Cadence _____ _____

Transpose this to the Key of A Minor. Write the rhythmic accent marks for $\frac{6}{8}$ time over the proper notes in each measure.

8 What is an OSTINATO or a GROUND bass? _____

_____

9 Name the MODES and give the letter-name for each *do*.

_____   _____

_____   _____

_____   _____

_____   _____

_____   _____

_____   _____

10 Write the letter-names for the two WHOLE-TONE SCALES.

_____   _____

Write the letter-names of the PENTATONIC SCALE and its transposition.

_____   _____

11 What is the other name for BINARY TIME? _____

Why is it called BINARY? _____

_____

What is the other name for TERNARY? _____

Why is it called TERNARY? _____

12 Name the 4 qualities of RHYTHM _____

_____

Index